4·45

STUDIES IN THE UK ECONOMY

Supply side economics

Rosalind Levačić

Lecturer in Economics
at the Open University

HEINEMANN
EDUCATIONAL

Heinemann Educational Books Ltd
Halley Court, Jordan Hill, Oxford OX2 8EJ

OXFORD LONDON EDINBURGH
MELBOURNE SYDNEY AUCKLAND
SINGAPORE MADRID IBADAN
NAIROBI GABORONE HARARE
KINGSTON PORTSMOUTH NH

First published 1988

British Library Cataloguing in Publication Data
Levačić, Rosalind
    Supply side economics. — (Studies in
    the UK economy).
    1. Great Britain. Economic policies.
    Role of supply-side economics
    I. Title II. Series
    330.941' 0858

ISBN 0 435 33004 7

Typeset and illustrated by Gecko Limited, Bicester, Oxon

Printed and bound in Great Britain by Biddles Ltd, King's Lynn and Guildford

Acknowledgements

Thanks are due to the following for permission to reproduce copyright
material: Centre for Economic Policy Research for the table on p.24;
Economics Association for the article on pp.52–3; *Financial Times* for the
articles on pp.3–4 and 29–31; The Controller of Her Majesty's Stationery
Office for the graphs on pp.7, 9, 10, 11, 15, 50 and the reports on pp.42–3
and 58; Ingram Pinn for the cartoon on p.20; Labour Party for the extract on
pp.62–3; National Institute of Economic and Social Research for the table on
p.14; Organisation of Economic Cooperation and Development for the
graphs on p.6 and the table on p.8; Social and Liberal Democrats for the
extract on pp.64–5.

Preface

This series aims to appeal to schools and colleges where both teachers and those taught are eager to get to grips with the real economy of the UK. *Supply Side Economics* applies micro and macro theory in an up-to-date way.

Traditional textbooks still give full coverage to the over-simple Keynesian diagrams universally taught in the 1960s. But the post-Keynesian world makes the inverted L-shaped aggregate demand curve look increasingly unrealistic. The world has changed and so has the quality of economic analysis. Unfortunately the response of text books is very lagged indeed!

Using diagrams and cleverly analytical data response questions integrated into the text, Rosalind Levačić explains the supply side – 'policies aimed at enhancing the performance of the UK economy' – as being built upon a micro framework that underpins the macro aggregate supply function. It is made into simplicity itself for pupils.

As is pointed out '(supply side economics) is not only an important topic in its own right, but a useful vehicle for revising one's knowledge of economics'.

Bryan Hurl
Series Editor

Contents

Chapter One

Introduction

The spread of supply side policies is a manifestation of a significant shift in ideas in the last decade.

Supply side economics is a term that came into widespread use in the 1980s to refer to a broad range of policies aimed at enhancing the performance of an economy by strengthening competitive market forces and improving economic incentives. These policies have been generally associated with governments of a conservative or right-wing bent – in particular the administrations of Ronald Reagan (1981–88) in the USA and Margaret Thatcher in the UK. But certain aspects of supply side policies have also been adopted by Labour governments, as in New Zealand and Australia. The spread of supply side policies is a manifestation of a significant shift in the last decade away from confidence in the efficiency of government intervention in the detailed workings of the economy. Instead the appropriate role of government is seen as setting the framework of rules, incentives and sanctions within which economic agents operate.

However, the apparent newness of supply side economics is deceptive. Since economics became a distinct area of study there has always been a great concern with the supply side of the economy – with the factors that determine the capacity of different economies to produce output and hence to improve living standards. The renewed interest in the 1980s in the supply side of the economy reflects two interrelated developments. One is a disenchantment with the Keynesian concentration on the control of aggregate demand as the major means whereby governments can regulate real national output. The other, already mentioned, is a decline of confidence in the ability of governments to improve economic growth by direct intervention – by running businesses, planning the economy or by directing investment into particular areas of production.

This short book explains the main features of supply side economics, using the term to refer to the set of ideas defined in the opening sentence. It relates supply side economic analysis to its associated policy measures, concentrating largely on those that have been adopted in the UK. Because supply side economics is such a wide-ranging topic all the basic principles of economic analysis can be brought to bear upon it. So it is not only an important topic in its own right, but also a useful vehicle for revising and integrating one's knowledge of economics.

Chapter 2 uses the concept of the *production function* to set out the determinants of an economy's capacity to supply output and of the growth in this capacity.

Chapter 3 then uses *microeconomic analysis* to investigate the roles of different types of economic agents – in particular producers and investors – operating within a market system. Supply side economists stress the importance of the incentives faced by economic agents in influencing their behaviour – in particular the desire to work – to accumulate capital and to take risks. These myriads of actions interact to determine the overall performance of the economy. Supply side economic policies are concerned to promote a growing, dynamic economy by operating on individual agents' incentives in appropriate ways; for example by reducing marginal rates of taxation and increasing the scope for competitive markets.

Chapter 4 sets out a *macroeconomic framework,* in the form of the aggregate demand and aggregate supply model, for relating supply side considerations to the determination of short-run output.

Chapter 5 examines the controversy between *Keynesians* and *monetarists* over appropriate macroeconomic policies, which stems from their different views as to how the aggregate supply of output responds to changes in demand.

Chapter 6 looks at *labour market policies* and relates their intended effects to overall economic performance using the macroeconomic framework of Chapters 4 and 5.

Chapter 7 concludes with a brief critique of supply side policies and indicates how their effectiveness needs to be assessed.

Data response question 1
Rising living standards

The purpose of this data response question is to alert you to the nature and significance of economic growth, the subject examined in the next chapter. First read the accompanying article from the *Financial Times* of March 1987.

1. What do you understand by the term 'standard of living'?

2. What evidence is there in the article of increased living standards in 1987 compared with 1957?
3. What, if anything, does evidence about changes in
   (a) the rate of inflation
   (b) unemployment
   (c) taxation
   indicate about improvements in living standards over time?

	Cost in 1957	Approx cost now	1957 cost adjusted for inflation
Average price of a house	£2170	£41150	£15632
1lb rump steak	5s 3½d	£3.50	£1.90
Large unsliced white loaf	7½d	45p	22p
Pint of milk	7d	25p	21p
First class postage	3d	18p	9p
Pint of beer	1s 4d	78p	48p
20 tipped cigarettes	2s 11d	£1.52	£1.04
Bottle of Scotch	£1 13s 4d	£7.80	£9.25
Gallon of petrol	5s 0d	£1.60	£1.79
Citroen 2CV	£598 7s 0d	£3094.64	£4300.66
Washing machine	£66 8s 6d	£250.00	£477.60
Cinema ticket	2s 6d	£2.30	88p
Return air-fare London/Paris	£15 10s	£156.00	£111.44
Electricity per kW hour	1½d	5.04p	5p
Gas per therm	1s 7d	38p	57p

Source: Consumers' Association

Change in living standards studied

THIRTY years ago the late Lord Stockton, when Prime Minister, made his memorable statement "Most of our people have never had it so good."

Yesterday the Consumers' Association, which was formed in 1957 to give independent advice on consumer products, took a look back at prices in 1957 to see how far living standards have changed during the intervening 30 years.

The association, in the latest issue of its magazine Which? points out that the present inflation rate of 3.7 per cent is below the 4 per cent experienced during 1957.

However unemployment, which

during 1957 fell from 380,000 to 335,000, has increased by almost 1,000 per cent in the subsequent 30 years.

Other statistics also show how far Britain has changed over three decades. For example, in 1957 the Japanese made one car for every 25 made in Britain. Now the position is reversed with the Japanese making 7.5 cars for every one made in Britain.

Average weekly earnings for a man in 1957 were about £12.10, the equivalent of £87 after adjustment for inflation. Currently average male earnings are actually £190 a week.

The working week has declined from 48.2 hours worked to 43.4 hours now.

However, the standard rate of income tax then was 42.5p in the pound, compared with the present rate of 29p in the pound.

Car ownership has risen from 24 per cent to 61 per cent while televisions are now found in 97 per cent of households, compared with 66 per cent in 1957.

The number of people taking holidays abroad has increased from 2m to 16m, while trade union membership is actually higher at 9.6m than the 8.3m in 1957.

The magazine points out that many of the things now taken for granted were not around in 1957. These include Access Cards, colour television, felt tipped pens, Jumbo jets, parking meters, wine boxes and yuppies.

David Churchill
Leisure Correspondent

Chapter Two

The determinants of economic growth

The factors that determine a country's rate of growth are highly complex, much debated and only imprecisely known.

Thirty years ago the UK's gross national product in real terms was half of what it was in 1987. *On average* over these years the UK economy grew at about 2.5 per cent a year, though this masks annual fluctuations which range from +8.2 to −2.8 per cent. However, other countries' economies grew faster and so living standards in Britain − measured as GDP per capita − though they doubled over this period, fell relative to other economies. In the early 1950s Britain had the third highest living standard in the world, but by the mid-1980s she ranked seventeenth. The realization of Britain's relatively poor economic performance has been widely perceived since the late 1950s. Then during the 1970s all economies experienced reductions in their rate of growth, as well as increasing inflation.

Some evidence for Britain's comparative economic performance is presented in Figures 1 and 2. From these (which are based on statistics from the Treasury and the OECD and CSO) you can see that Britain's comparative performance has recently improved, and that growth rates since the trough of the last recession in 1981 are higher than in the 1970s.

The factors that determine a country's rate of growth are highly complex, much debated and only imprecisely known. However, by categorizing the different sources of growth, we can begin to understand the relevant factors and how they might be affected by government action.

The production function
The key factors of production in determining the rate of growth of output are the quantity and quality of the **capital stock** and the **labour force**. The production process consists of organizing and combining labour and capital services to add value to the input of intermediate goods, such as raw materials, energy and components. The value added in the productive process depends on the quantity and quality of labour and capital.

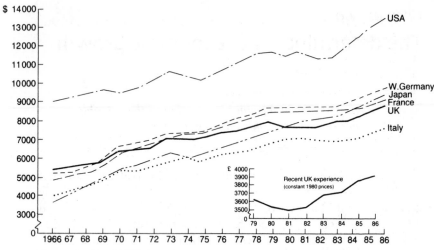

Figure 1 Real GDPs per head at constant 1980 $ prices (purchasing-power parity basis)

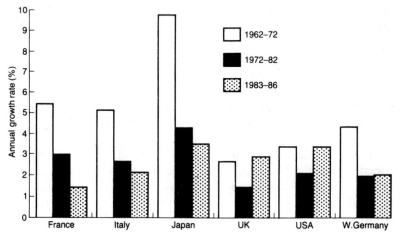

Figure 2 Rate of growth of real GDP, 1962–87

The quality of capital is improved over time by discovering and applying new knowledge about technology. **Technical progress** also changes the skills required by the labour force, as well as the kinds of goods and services that can be produced.

The relationship between output and the factors that determine the amount that can be supplied is called the **production function**. This states that the quantity of output (value added to raw materials, etc.) produced depends on

- the quantity of labour employed
- the quantity of capital
- the level of technical knowledge.

Productivity

The level of technical knowledge possessed and successfully deployed in an economy is crucial in determining the quality of the labour force and of the capital stock. It is an important determinant of how productive is a unit of labour or of capital. The **productivity** of a unit of labour is the amount of value added output produced divided by the number of units of labour used to produce that output. It is known as the **average product of labour.** The average product of capital is, in principle, measured in the same way.

The average product of a worker will be higher the more units of capital he or she has to work with and the more productive is that capital. Labour productivity is easier to measure than the productivity of the capital stock because it is difficult to measure capital. This is why labour productivity is so frequently used to compare the perform-ance of economies and to monitor their progress over time. Figure 3 shows how output per head of the labour force in manufacturing has grown in the last twenty years in the UK and four other countries (figures from NEDO and CSO). The UK now has the lowest output per head in manufacturing of the five countries.

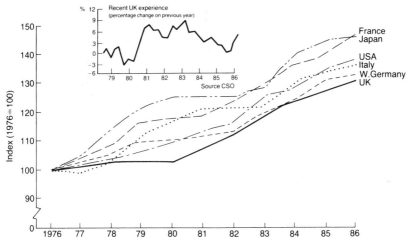

Figure 3   Labour productivity: output per person hour in manufacturing

Although Britain's labour productivity grew over the post-war period, other countries' output per head grew more rapidly than Britain's. As Japan has experienced a much higher rate of growth of labour productivity, its output per worker overtook Britain's in the late 1970s.

The different performances of economies in terms of their rates of growth of labour productivity are given in Table 1, which is based on a Treasury report (OECD data). This shows the annual average rate of increase in output per worker in manufacturing and in the whole economy, for the seven major industrialized countries. You should note the changes in the UK's performance over time as well as in comparison with other countries. Removing the effects of the 1980–81 recession, labour productivity in manufacturing in the UK grew at 5.4 per cent between 1981 and 1986.

Table 1 Growth in labour productivity in the seven major industrialized countries, 1964–86

	Manufacturing			Whole economy		
	1964–73	1973–79	1979–86	1964–73	1973–79	1979–86
Canada	4.3	2.5	3.0	2.5	0.5	0.6
France	5.4	3.0	2.5	4.5	2.8	1.5
W.Germany	3.9	3.3	2.3	4.2	2.9	1.4
Italy	5.5	2.5	2.4	5.6	1.7	1.0
Japan	9.8	4.0	2.7	7.4	2.9	2.8
UK	3.8	0.7	3.5	2.7	1.1	1
USA	3.4	3.5	2.3	1.6	0.2	0.7
Averages	5.0	3.2	2.5	3.6	1.5	1.3

For labour productivity to grow over time there has to be either
- an increase in the capital stock
  and/or
- technical progress by which improved knowledge is acquired and used to increase the productivity of the capital stock and the skills of the labour force.

The physical quantity of capital can only be increased by **investment.** This requires that some current resources are not devoted to consumption but are saved and transformed into capital goods to be used for producing more goods and services in the future. This process is known as **capital accumulation.**

However, there is no direct relationship between the proportion of its national output that a country invests and its rate of growth, because it is not only the *amount* of investment that is important but

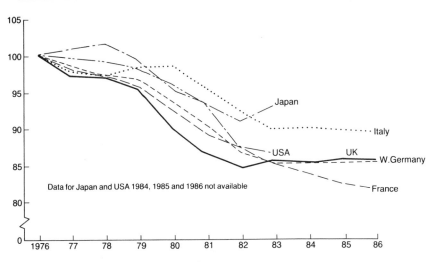

Figure 4 GDP per unit of capital (measured in national currency for the whole economy at constant 1980 prices)

also its *quality*. An indication of the quality of a country's investment is obtained by estimating the average amount of output produced per unit of capital. This measure is called the **output–capital ratio**. A low output–capital ratio indicates low capital productivity. Figure 4, which is based on NEDO data, shows that the UK's output–capital ratio is relatively low compared with the other major industrialized countries, though it has improved its position since the early 1980s.

Investment in the capital stock – in the form of plant, machinery and infrastructure – is not the only form of investment. Investment in research and development is also required in order to develop and diffuse new technical knowledge and improve the productivity of capital and labour. Figure 5, also based on NEDO data, gives some indication of the amount the UK spends on research and development compared with other countries.

Similarly, education and training of the labour force requires investment because resources are devoted to these tasks instead of to immediate consumption. Hence the quantity and the quality of investment in both capital and labour is crucial in determining economic growth.

International competitiveness

A country's economic progress cannot be considered in isolation from other countries which provide a competitive stimulus. Labour productivity is one of the key factors in determining how well a country's

9

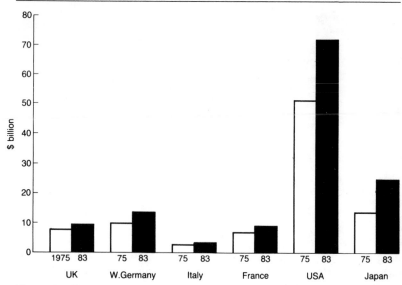

Figure 5 Gross expenditure on R&D at constant 1980 $ prices (purchasing-power parity basis)

products compete on international markets against the products of other countries. To be competitive a firm's product must be priced at or below the prices of substitutes of similar quality produced by rival suppliers.

The price a firm can charge and still make adequate profits depends on the cost per unit of its output. This in turn depends on the cost of the labour and capital required to produce a unit of output. The labour cost of a unit of output (its **unit labour cost**) depends on two factors:

- *The amount a firm has to pay for labour.* This depends not only on the wage rate but also on the other costs of employing labour – social security contributions and non-pecuniary benefits such as holidays and pleasant working conditions.
- *Labour productivity.* The higher the average product of labour the lower are unit labour costs, since the cost per week of employing a worker is spread over a larger quantity of output.

We can express all this as an equation:

$$\text{Unit labour cost} = \frac{\text{Wage} + \text{non-wage costs per worker}}{\text{Average product per worker}}$$

So a country with a relatively low level of labour productivity can still be competitive internationally if it pays sufficiently low wages. But if a

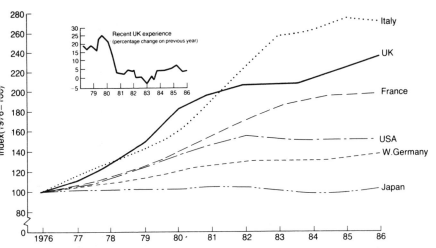

Figure 6 Labour costs per unit of output in manufacturing, in local currency

country's wages rise more rapidly than its labour productivity then its labour costs per unit of output increase over time. Particularly in the years 1972–82, Britain's relatively low rate of productivity growth combined with a relatively high rate of wage inflation made for a relatively high rate of increase in unit labour costs. Figure 6 (NEDO data again) shows how unit labour costs have risen in the UK compared with its main competitors.

A country becomes less competitive internationally if its unit labour costs rise faster than those of other countries. This loss in competitiveness can be countered by allowing the **exchange rate** to depreciate, so reducing the price of the domestic countries' goods in terms of foreign exchange. The problem with this strategy is that depreciation of the currency raises the domestic price of imported goods and so increases the country's rate of inflation.

Relative unit labour costs, taking into account changes in countries' exchange rates, are shown in Figure 7 (copied from an article by V.Rossi *et al.*). Relative unit labour costs vary owing to the combined effects of changes in

- labour productivity
- wage and non-wage costs of employing a unit of labour
- exchange rates.

The rise in the UK's relative unit labour costs between 1977 and 1981 (and especially in 1980–81) was due in part to an appreciating exchange rate – which has since depreciated.

11

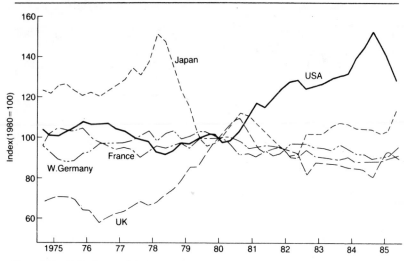

Figure 7 Relative unit labour costs

Supply side policies seek to improve the growth rate of the economy and its international competitiveness by operating on the factors that determine the productivity of labour and capital as well as on those that influence the cost of labour and capital. In terms of the production possibility curve, depicted in Figure 8 for a simplified economy consisting of just two goods, supply side policies are concerned with

- moving out towards the production possibility curve by increasing efficiency
- shifting the production possibility curve itself outwards and so raising **productive capacity.**

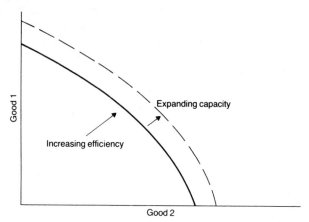

Figure 8 The production possibility curve

KEY WORDS	
Capital stock	Capital accumulation
Labour force	Output–capital ratio
Technical progress	International competitiveness
Production function	Unit labour cost
Productivity	Exchange rate
Average product of labour	Relative unit labour cost
Investment	Productive capacity

Reading list
NEDO, *British Industrial Performance and International Competitiveness Over Recent Years*, 1987.
Wigley, P., 'The impact of technical innovation', *Economic Review*,

Essay Topics
1. What factors determine a country's rate of economic growth?
2. What is the role of investment in determining a country's rate of economic growth?
3. What is meant by a country's economic competitiveness? What are the strengths and limitations of 'relative unit labour costs in manufacturing' as an indicator of international competitiveness?
4. Why have Britain's relative unit labour costs remained high compared with those of its major competitors? What factors explain the improved trend in Britain's relative unit labour costs in the 1980s?

Data response question 2

Unit costs in manufacturing

The following table (from an article by G.F. Ray) gives data in the form of an index in which the UK is valued at 100 in each year, so that labour costs and labour productivity in the other countries can be compared in each year. All the variables are measured in a common currency so that changes in exchange rates are already taken into account.

1. Are hourly labour costs, labour productivity and unit labour costs higher or lower in the UK than in the other countries?
2. For each of the variables, state whether the UK's relative performance has improved or worsened since 1980.
3. Why does the UK have relatively low hourly labour costs and relatively high unit labour costs?
4. The accompanying graph shows the variations of UK cost contributions (NEDO data), which are sources of changes in UK cost competitiveness in manufacturing. What factors explain the behaviour of relative unit labour costs depicted in the graph?

	Total hourly labour costs*			Labour productivity (output per hour)			Unit labour costs†		
	1980	1984	1986	1980	1984	1986	1980	1984	1986
USA	126	194	161	273	262	267	46	74	60
Japan	80	109	129	196	177	176	41	62	73
France	121	114	122	193	179	184	63	64	66
W.Germany	165	153	173	255	232	178	65	66	97
Italy	108	117	127	173	156	155	62	75	82
Belguim	176	140	149	207	200	154	85	70	97
Netherlands	160	142	156	269	267	205	59	53	76

* This includes all social charges.
† Refer back to the equation for calculating unit labour cost, and then check a few of these figures.

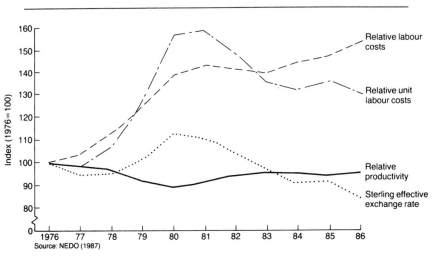

Source: NEDO (1987)

Chapter Three

Supply side microeconomics

The supply side approach emphasizes the importance of individual economic agents motivated by self-interest.

The rationale of supply side policies

While the observation that economic growth depends on the quantity and quality of investment in capital and labour is a valuable insight, it is only the beginning of the quest for answers to the conundrum of why some nations make faster economic progress than others.

The supply side approach emphasizes the importance of individual **economic agents** motivated by self-interest and reacting to the incentives and sanctions provided by the economic system within which they operate. In this, supply side economics draws upon a long tradition, extending back to Adam Smith's *Wealth of Nations,* and revitalized by the more recent ideas of Hayek and the Austrian school. The latter stress the vital function of competitive markets in providing people with the incentives to seek out information about profitable opportunities for production and exchange. In terms of Figure 8, the production possibility curve is not known. Information concerning the most efficient methods of production and which goods are most valued by consumers will only be discovered by economic agents with a personal incentive to do so because they expect to benefit as a consequence.

The key economic agents on the supply side of the economy are the various categories of producers – entrepreneurs, managers and workers – together with investors (those people who are postponing consumption by investing in productive assets) and their advisers, the financial institutions. According to the supply side view, entrepreneurs are motivated by the expectation of profit to discover and supply products that consumers want and to use efficient production methods. The stimulus to serve consumers is best provided in competitive markets. If there are few rival suppliers to whom consumers can turn if dissatisfied, then firms can still earn profits even while operating with costs above the feasible miminum and while failing to produce the type and quality of goods consumers prefer. Without the stimulus of competition a firm has less inducement to organize its workforce efficiently and to provide its employees with incentives to work efficiently and to satisfy customers' wants.

The supply side's disbelief in the ability of governments to improve economic performance by means of direct intervention is based on the argument that governments cannot obtain the requisite information about the most efficient ways of allocating resources. The market is more efficient at discovering and transmitting such information because it relies on specialists in particular market niches obtaining and using information about the kinds of goods and services demanded by consumers and about the cheapest methods of production. The economy is in a constant state of flux as changes occur in technical knowledge, in the prices of raw materials, or in consumer tastes. An economy is *dynamic,* in the sense that it continually generates new applications for technical knowledge and adapts rapidly and smoothly to changes in the forces of demand and supply, if individual economic agents have the appropriate incentives. In this view the role of government is to ensure that the laws, regulations and institutions operate so as to provide economic agents with the required incentives and information. Direct intervention by government – whereby *it* determines which goods should be produced, where investment should be directed, which areas of research should be investigated or what prices should be charged – is doomed to be inefficient. Governments cannot obtain the requisite information at the right time and are pressured by special interest groups to allocate resources to satisfy their own specific interests.

The rationale of supply side policies is derived directly from this view of how markets operate in allocating resources, in contrast to the comparative inefficiency of government regulation. Critics of supply side policies hold a different set of opinions regarding the efficacy of the market system. The market is seen to fail in many instances, and government action is required to spur investment and innovation and to strengthen the ability of firms to compete.

The general aim of supply side policies is to strengthen and extend competitive market forces and to alter existing laws and regulations in order to improve the incentives for individuals to seek out productive activities.

Promoting competition by deregulation

A regulated market is one in which laws, and the related regulations that authorized bodies make, limit the actions of producers and consumers. These regulations are often justified as being needed to protect customers and workers from the consequences of their inadequate information about the quality of goods or hazards of working conditions. All markets are regulated by health and safety laws and consumer protection legislation, but many have or have had specific regulations which limit competition and act in the interests of established suppliers.

Deregulation involves reducing the number of regulations by removing those that serve only to restrict competition and do little to enhance the safety of customers or workers. The objectives of deregulation are to increase competition between existing suppliers and between them and new suppliers who can now enter the market. This should reduce costs and stimulate the provision of new services for which there is a demand. Recent examples of deregulation in the UK are buses and the Stock Exchange.

The 1980 Transport Act deregulated long-distance coach travel. Licence restrictions on operators entering the market were removed and limited to safety standards. Many small companies entered the market which was dominated by the then state-owned National Bus Company. This fought back successfully, cutting fares and introducing new routes. There has been a significant fall in long-distance coach fares and a consequent rise in the number of passenger-miles travelled. In 1986 local bus services were deregulated. Until then private operators had been unable to enter the market without securing a local authority licence for the route. Under the new legislation local authorities are required to tender for their local bus routes and award the tender to the cheapest contractor. Subsidies to bus services have also been cut. The objective of the legislation is to reduce the costs of bus travel and to provide those services for which there is a local demand by allowing the entry of small operators.

The Stock Exchange operated practices which limited competition. It had a system of fixed commissions for buying and selling shares, so that all firms charged the same agreed price. Another restriction was *single capacity* – jobbers (firms holding shares and bonds in order to make a market in them) had to be separate from stockbrokers (firms who bought and sold securities on behalf of investors); single capacity therefore limited the entry of financial institutions into the Stock Exchange. When the Office of Fair Trading threatened legal action against fixed commissions, the Stock Exchange agreed to abandon fixed commissions voluntarily in return for exemption from prosecution for restrictive practices. The much publicized Big Bang of October 1986 marked the day on which the Stock Exchange introduced computerized trading, *dual capacity* and variable commissions. These changes ushered in considerable restructuring of city financial institutions, the entry of many foreign firms and a considerable growth in financial activity.

Other areas which have been deregulated are opticians, house conveyancing and telecommunications.

Promoting competition by privatization

Privatization in the form of selling state-owned assets to the private sector can promote competition if such a transfer of ownership is accompanied by deregulation or the breaking up of a state monopoly into several smaller businesses. The best example of such a privatization is that of the National Bus Company, which in the course of 1986–87 was gradually sold off as separate companies, many of them to management buyout groups. However the bulk of the large-scale privatizations – British Telecom, British Gas, British Airways and the British Airports Authority – have involved the transfer intact of a state monopoly or dominant firm to the private sector. This has been much criticized as doing little to promote competition and therefore efficiency. The government is currently investigating the best way to privatize the electricity industry quickly, while at the same time encouraging competition and investment.

Some privatizations have been accompanied by deregulation, but then it is the latter that actually promotes competition. For instance the privatization of British Telecom in 1985 was preceded by the 1981 Telecommunications Act which permitted certain kinds of private equipment to be connected to the British Telecom network and allowed a newly formed private consortium, Mercury, to compete. Mercury is installing optical fibre cables for business communications which it connects with the BT network. As a result of the 1981 Act new products, such as car telephones and more sophisticated receivers, have mushroomed.

The privatization programme has served purposes other than straight supply side efficiency. It has, for example, extended share ownership and financed the government budget deficit. These and other aspects of privatization are discussed by Bryan Hurl in a companion text in this series, *Privatization and the public sector.*

Taxation

Taxation is an important issue for supply-siders because almost all taxes alter peoples' incentives. Lump-sum taxes do not alter incentives because the amount paid does not vary with a taxpayer's actions in earning income or in investing or spending it. The government's

Cartoon by Ingram Pinn from the *Financial Times* 22 April 1988

intention is to replace local authority domestic rates by a community charge, a fixed sum payable in full by all adults with some exceptions such as those on supplementary benefit. However, as the tax system is intended not only to finance government spending but also to redistribute income by taxing people according to their ability to pay, there is very limited scope for lump-sum taxation.

Disincentives

Whether a tax is levied according to a person's ability to pay or according to his or her expenditure, it reduces the rate of return that individual obtains from market activities – like working for a wage or investing in shares or other assets with taxable yields. The supply side argument is that, as a consequence of taxation, people will engage in less market activity overall, as well as shift into those market activities that are less heavily taxed. They will also risk not reporting all their income to the tax authorities; in other words they will work in the **black economy.**

The more extreme supply side economists have maintained that the proportion of national income taken in tax is too high and that reducing this proportion would stimulate economic growth. There is little empirical evidence to support this contention at such a high level of aggregation or for levels of taxation that have actually been experienced. As Figure 9 shows, there has in the past been little relationship between the proportion of a country's national income that is taxed and its growth rate. Ronald Reagan (President of the USA from 1981 to 1988) was utterly convinced of the necessity for reducing taxes – reportedly a conviction gained when, as a Hollywood film star, he found that it was not worth making more than three films a year because of tax liabilities. The Economic Recovery Tax Act in 1981 cut US federal income tax rates by 23 per cent over a three-year period. The Thatcher governments have been far more cautious: tax revenue as a proportion of national income actually rose under the Conservatives from 34 to 38 per cent – and only began to fall in 1984.

Concern about the inefficiency caused by the *structure* of the tax system, rather than about the level of taxes, is far more widespread and has stimulated tax reforms in the 1980s in a large number of countries. By the **tax structure** is meant the different kinds of activities that are taxed and the differential tax rates applied. For example, what kind of income is taxed and what rates of tax different income earners have to pay are elements of the tax structure.

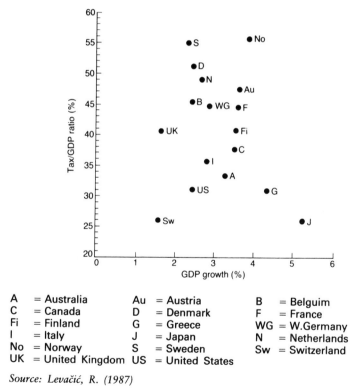

A   = Australia   Au = Austria   B   = Belguim
C   = Canada   D   = Denmark   F   = France
Fi = Finland   G   = Greece   WG = W.Germany
I   = Italy   J   = Japan   N   = Netherlands
No = Norway   S   = Sweden   Sw = Switzerland
UK = United Kingdom US = United States

Source: Levačić, R. (1987)

Figure 9   An international comparison of growth rates and tax/GDP ratios (GDP growth is the annual average rate between 1970 and 1982; the tax/GDP percentage is the average for 1972, 1977 and 1982)

Distortion

Taxes distort choices. If a good is taxed more heavily than others, consumers will buy less of it and switch to other goods. This reduces consumers' utility because they would prefer, in the absence of the tax, to buy more of the good.

This consideration is particularly pertinent for the taxation of income from investment, since the tax structure has resulted in huge differences in the post-tax rate of return from investing in different kinds of assets. Mortgage interest tax relief increases the private rate of return from investing in a house compared with investing in a business. Tax relief on premiums for life assurance and pension contributions has meant that individuals get a better return from saving via life assurance and pension fund schemes than by investing directly in shares. Until 1988, capital gains were taxed more lightly than income from investment, especially when investment income prior to 1979 was subject to a maximum marginal rate of 98 per cent. Such differential tax treatment of assets distort investment choice by inducing investors to seek capital gains – by buying works of art, for instance, rather than company shares.

Supply side policies aim to remove such distortions by simplifying the tax structure, by reducing the number of tax exemptions and having fewer variations in tax rates for different items and for different classes of taxpayers. The supply side concern with the distortionary and disincentive effects of taxation has underpinned tax reform in the 1980s in the UK, the USA and many other economies.

Taxation of earned income

One of the most firmly held supply side views is that income tax is a disincentive to work and, in particular, that high *marginal* rates of tax discourage both the earning and reporting of income to such an extent that cutting tax rates in fact *increases* rather than *diminishes* tax revenues. The argument that high marginal tax rates are a disincentive to work is more readily conceded than the view that the problem is a high *level* of taxation. This can be deduced from a straightforward application of economic theory.

Let us take the case of an increase in the higher rate of income tax from 60 to 80 per cent. An affected individual experiences a drop in his or her disposable income. This is the **income effect** of the increase in taxation. Had this loss come about instead from the imposition of a lump-sum tax the individual might choose to work harder to make up the income, and the extra income would be kept. However, since the tax in question is an income tax, the individual can now keep only 20 per cent of any additional income earned, not 40 per cent. This makes leisure, which is the alternative way of spending time, relatively cheaper and hence more attractive. Thus income tax has a **substitution effect**: a rise in the rate of income tax makes leisure time cheaper relative to work time because the opportunity cost of leisure in the form of income foregone is now less. The substitution effect of a fall in price of any *good* is to increase the demand for it. The substitution effect of *income tax* increases the demand for leisure and so reduces the number of hours of work individuals are willing to do.

The *total effect* of an increase in income tax is the sum of the income effect (which increases the supply of working hours) and the substitution effect (which reduces the supply of working hours). The net effect will be a reduction in work if the substitution effect is larger than the income effect.

The policy conclusion to be drawn from this analysis is that high **marginal rates of tax** are more likely to be a disincentive to work than a high average rate of tax. Indeed a high average rate of tax accompanied by lower marginal rates may well stimulate work effort through the income effect.

There has been much government rhetoric on its success in cutting income tax rates, but it has drawn less attention to the fact that value-added tax (VAT) and National Insurance contributions were raised to offset revenue losses. The Conservative government made its first major supply side tax changes in its 1979 Budget. The basic rate of income tax was cut from 33 to 30 per cent and the top rate of income tax was reduced from 83 to 60 per cent. At the same time VAT rates were raised (from 8 to 15 per cent for many non-essentials). National Insurance contributions were later raised and, in 1985, graduated National Insurance contributions were introduced. (Previously all employees had paid the same rate between lower and upper income bands.) Further cuts were made in the basic rate of income tax – to 27 per cent and 25 per cent in 1987 and 1988 respectively. With the 1987 general election won, the top marginal rate of tax was reduced in the next Budget from 60 to 40 per cent.

Table 2 shows an estimate of the impact of the government's tax measures on the *overall* marginal rate of tax paid by an average worker in income tax, VAT and National Insurance contributions. This shows that it is misleading merely to focus on income tax changes. The overall marginal rate of tax in fact rose under the Conservatives and did not fall below the rate inherited from the previous Labour government until 1986.

The reduction in the marginal rates faced by high earners has been

Table 2 Marginal percentage tax rates for a worker on average earnings

Year	VAT*	Income tax	NI (employee's)	NI (employer's)	Totals†
1978–79	4.85	33.0	6.50	12.75	48.8
1979–80	8.25	30.0	6.50	13.50	48.3
1980–81	8.25	30.0	6.75	13.70	48.6
1981–82	8.25	30.0	7.75	13.70	49.4
1982–83	8.25	30.0	8.75	13.70	50.2
1983–84	8.25	30.0	9.00	11.95	49.7
1984–85	8.25	30.0	9.00	10.45	49.4
1985–86	8.25	30.0	9.00	10.45	49.0
1986–87	8.25	29.0	9.00	10.45	48.1
1987–88	8.25	27.0	9.00	10.45	46.5

* The VAT rate here is calculated from the proportion of consumer-good purchases which carry VAT, multiplied by the current VAT rate.
† The total tax rate on labour is calculated as the private purchasing power of the worker as a percentage of the employer's cash paid out.

Source: Matthews and Minford (1987)

more dramatic. A person paying the top tate of tax on earned income faced a marginal income tax rate of 83 per cent in the 1970s compared with 40 per cent in the late 1980s. However, it may well be the top earners who respond to tax cuts in the way supply-siders envisage. It is argued that Britain's top marginal tax rates should not exceed those in comparable economies in order to induce high income earners to work here.

Evidence on the effect of tax on work incentives is contentious and incomplete. What *is* available suggests that for male *average* income earners the effect is very weak, though stronger for married women. This is probably because married women choose between working (usually part-time) and doing unpaid domestic work, and so are more influenced in their choice of how to spend their marginal time by their after-tax wage.

There is somewhat stronger evidence that high income workers respond to tax cuts by earning more and/or declaring more of their income to the tax authorities. A study of the 1982–84 tax cuts in the USA estimated that personal incomes were about 2 per cent higher as a result of the tax cuts, and that, as a consequence, total income tax revenues fell 25 per cent *less* than they would have done without this induced increase in incomes. Furthermore, the high income earners – who had their top marginal tax rates cut from 70 to 50 per cent by the

1981 Tax Act – increased their incomes sufficiently to pay more in tax than they had at the higher tax rate.

The UK evidence is more circumstantial. The top 5 per cent of earners increased their share of national income by 10 per cent between 1979–80 and 1984–85 (from 15.6 to 17.2 per cent) but their tax payments increased by 11.5 per cent (from 23.4 per cent of tax revenue to 26.1 per cent). This increase in the relative income of the top earners could have been due to tax cuts; but it could also be attributed to other factors, such as high unemployment amongst manual workers which has widened income differentials.

Social security benefits

Another supply side argument is that social security benefits discourage work by low income earners. The higher the benefits received when unemployed relative to income from working, the less incentive there is for people to seek work. This is a controversial argument because it can imply policies to cut the incomes of those who are already poor. There is disagreement too amongst economists about the empirical evidence regarding the strength of the disincentive effect of social security benefits. The majority opinion is that there is *some* disincentive effect but that it is weak and can explain only a little of the high unemployment experienced in the 1980s.

Taxation of capital

Here this includes the taxation of businesses, since income is derived from the ownership of assets vested in a business or from lending to businesses. Taxation affects the incentives of producers in various ways. Supply-siders argue that high tax rates on investment income discourage capital accumulation by reducing the rate of return on investment. This is likely to be a particular problem for small and growing businesses which have difficulty in raising finance and which rely for share capital on ploughing back profits or on a few outside equity holders.

Taxation measures to encourage the development of small businesses include a reduced rate of corporation tax for small firms, grants for people to set up their own business, subsidized loans, and tax relief for individuals investing in businesses not quoted on the Stock Exchange. Small businesses have been much favoured by the current government as engines for a dynamic economy; they are seen as flexible and well motivated because they are run by owner-entrepreneurs who are keen to seek out new business opportunities, to expand and to provide employment. Sceptics point to the high failure rate of small businesses. Though they have grown in numbers and in the proportion of employment they provide, doubt is expressed as to their ability to absorb the labour shed by large firms since 1980.

Tax relief has been introduced on profit-sharing schemes whereby employees' incomes are linked to their company's profitability. These schemes are encouraged on the grounds that they improve the performance of managers and workers by giving them a direct stake in the fortunes of the business.

Concluding remarks

This chapter has given a broad overview of supply side policies with respect to taxation and competition. Supply side policies for the labour market are considered in Chapter 6. As supply side measures are micro-level policies they are necessarily highly varied and detailed. The data response question for this chapter provides further examples of supply side policies and asks you to relate them to supply side economic analysis.

```
                          KEY WORDS

  Economic agents           Distortion
  Deregulation              Income effect
  Privatization             Substitution effect
  Disincentives             Marginal rates of tax
  Black economy             Average rate of tax
  Tax structure
```

Reading list

Foreman-Peck, J., 'Natural monopoly and telecommunications', *Economic Review*, September 1986.

Greenhalgh, C., 'The determinants of labour supply', *Economic Review*, January 1987.

Levačić, R., *Economic Policy Making*, Chapter 5, Wheatsheaf, 1987.

Matthews, K. and Minford, P., 'Mrs Thatcher's economic policies 1979–87', *Economic Policy*, October 1987.

Robins, P., 'Government policy: taxation and supply side economics', *Economics,* No. 98, summer 1987.

Smith, D., *Mrs Thatcher's economics,* Heinemann Educational Books, 1988.

Storey, D., 'The performance of small firms', *Economic Review*, September 1987.

Thomas, W.A., 'Big Bang and the City', *Economic Review*, May 1987.

Essay topics

1. What are the economic advantages and disadvantages associated with a reduction in the basic rate of income tax?
   Oxford and Cambridge Schools Examination Board, June 1987
2. It has been suggested that the incentive to work in the UK will be increased by (a) a reduction in social security payments, and (b) a reduction in the higher rates of taxation. Explain and evaluate the reasoning underlying these views.
   Joint Matriculation Board, June 1986
3. 'We need to strengthen incentives, by allowing people to keep more of what they earn.' (Sir Geoffrey Howe, Budget speech, 1979). Give a broad outline of the UK tax system and say whether or not you agree with this statement.
   Joint Matriculation Board, June 1985
4. What is meant by 'economic efficiency'? What effect, if any, is the privatization of large sections of the public sector likely to exert on the efficiency of the economy?
   Joint Matriculation Board, June 1986
5. With reference to recent experience, examine the economic arguments for and against privatization.
   University of London Schools Examinations Board, June 1986

Data response question 3

Supply side measures

Consider each of the following supply side measures, all of which were introduced in the 1980s. Indicate which factors in the production function each measure is likely to affect, and why. What do you think is the supply side justification for the measure? Think of possible drawbacks to it.

- The Business Expansion Scheme was first introduced as the Business Start-up Scheme in 1981; the 1983 Budget extended the idea as the BES. Individuals can claim tax relief at their top marginal rate on equity investments in eligible existing unquoted trading companies.
- Under the Loan Guarantee Scheme the government guarantees 80 per cent of approved bank loans to small businesses, up to a ceiling amount, and for a 3 per cent premium on the guaranteed portion of the loan.
- A Small Engineering Firms Investment Scheme was revived in 1983, initially for three years, to provide grants to engineering businesses to buy advanced machine tools.

- The Enterprise Allowance Scheme helps unemployed people set up in business by providing them with a small weekly cash grant for a year.
- Small companies pay a reduced rate of corporation tax.
- Corporation tax relief for investment was abolished in 1984. This was announced in the Budget and explained by the government in the following terms:

> 'Tax incentives for investment are considered to have encouraged projects with low or even negative pre-tax profitability, so that the quality of investment has suffered and uneconomic investment has been supported at the expense of jobs.
>
> The incentives for plant and machinery and industrial building will be reduced in three annual stages . . . .After 31 March 1986 there will be no first-year allowance and all expenditure on plant and machinery will qualify for annual allowances on a 25% reducing balance basis.'
> (*Economic Progress Report* No. 166, March/April 1984)

At the same time corporation tax was reduced in stages from 50 per cent in 1983–84 to 35 per cent in 1986–87.

- Investment income surcharge was abolished in 1984. This had been a tax on unearned income of an additional 15 per cent on top of the taxpayer's highest income tax rate.
- Tax relief on life assurance premiums was abolished in 1984.
- Capital transfer tax (on wealth given to others) was reduced in the 1984 Budget and abolished in the 1986 Budget. It was replaced by Inheritance Tax.
- Stamp duty on land, building and share transactions was reduced from 2 to 1 per cent in 1984 and further cut to 0.5 per cent in 1986.
- Personal equity plans were announced in the 1986 Budget with effect from 1987. Individuals can invest up to £3000 a year in equities and not pay tax on the dividends or capital gains.
- Capital duty (a 1 per cent levy on companies raising new capital) was abolished in 1988.
- Government grants are available to private-sector firms for research and development in microelectronics.

Data response question 4
Entrepreneurs ring the changes in telecommunications

Read the accompanying article from the *Financial Times* of 15 June 1987. Which of the supply side measures mentioned in data response question 3 or discussed in this chapter do you think could have helped these businessmen? Discuss how important you think such measures are in determining the success of a new business, compared with other factors.

Entrepreneurs ring the changes in telecommunications

MR STEPHEN HOLMES is a millionaire and he is not yet 30. Yet in 1981 he had to go to his father to borrow the £100 he needed to buy a couple of telephone answering machines, one for sale, the other for rental.

Thanks to the success of Dial A Phone, his Manchester-based company, he can now boast a Rolls-Royce and a mansion in Derbyshire.

Mr Graham Thomas was president of Cardiff University Conservative Club when Mr Neil Kinnock, now Labour Party leader, headed the university's Labour Club. Today, Mr Thomas drives a Rolls with the number plate 1 GRA and sponsors horse trials.

All that is due to the Carphone Group, his Somerset based company, which is heading for turnover of £30m this year.

Mr Bob Old did not know what a telephone answering machine was when he gave up being an army helicopter pilot in 1979. Three years later, he started selling machines in Wetherby, where his company, Rocom, is based.

Sales of all types of telecommunications equipment last year reached £14m and Mr Old expects comfortably to be a millionaire when he takes Rocom to the market in a few years.

Mr Robin Bailey, with a PhD in engineering, is also entering the millionaire league. Five years ago, he was part of a 12-strong company making microcomputer add-ons in a mews in Swiss Cottage, London.

In 1983, he helped form National Telephone Systems, now based in London's Docklands area and with sales of more than £10m, by designing a new private telephone exchange.

Mr Richard O'Dell-Poulden abandoned management consultancy in 1982 to start Dellfield, a company making private telephone exchanges in Stroud, Gloucestershire.

He still remembers the "tremendous experience of walking into a bare building and not even having a photocopier." Dellfield is aiming for £7m sales this year and is selling its product in the Far East.

These five people have widely different backgrounds, yet share one thing: liberalisation in the telecommunications has helped them become wealthy.

Opening UK telecommunications to competition is often seen solely in terms of the epic struggle between British Telecom and Mercury Communications, its network rival. Yet equally importantly it has also stimulated entrepreneurs to enter a market traditionally the preserve of the big boys.

They had the nous to spot opportunities created by freer competition. As Mr O'Dell-Poulden puts it: "Any market which liberalises gets turned on its head, whether its private exchanges, airlines or monkey glands. In that situation, small companies can prosper – and they have."

The new entrants span the telecommunications industry: they are in

29

manufacturing, distribution, dealing, retailing, installation, maintenance and in the new value added services being sent over the public telephone networks.

Most of the newcomers, however, have steered clear of design and manufacturing – National Telephone Systems and Dellfield are exceptions – reflecting the tendency, widely seen as the most disappointing feature of telecommunications liberalisation in the UK, for most new equipment to come from abroad.

Mr Mel Ziziros, whose consultancy, MZA, watches the liberalising market, says: "Most of the activity has been distribution because the entry costs are so much lower."

Mr Holmes in Manchester needed just his father's £100 to start his business and Mr Old in Wetherby financed all Rocom's growth internally, not asking for so much as a bank overdraft.

Some of the new telecommunications entrepreneurs had earlier tried their luck at other businesses. For others, liberalisation gave them the chance to stop being a hired hand.

Mr Thomas had already made and lost a pile of money in the property boom of the early 1970s before he started a mobile communications business in 1978. However, Mr Thomas's big break in telecommunications came after 1985 when his company, Carphone, quickly became a leading independent distributor in the new and booming cellular telephone market.

Mr Holmes, by contrast, had been a representative for Telephone Rentals, the long-established publicly-quoted distribution company, when he realised that liberalisation gave him the chance to branch out on his own.

Ironically, many of these budding businessmen found the liberalised telecommunications regime a problem when they started up. Most denounce the quirks in the early arrangements for approving new equipment and of the behaviour of

British Telecom in trying to hold on to its monopoly.

Mr Bailey at National Telephone Systems recalls: "In the early days, there was a period of about a year in which we could make no headway in getting our product approved."

Mr Thomas says: "The early years were not easy because British Telecom used every trick in the book to keep out competition. Things are easier now they recognise they are a company which does not have a god-given right to exist."

These entrepreneurs still gripe about the regime, although they all accept it has improved. Mr Old reckons the approvals procedure is subject to long delays and is biased against innovative equipment because it tests equipment against specifications written in advance by the approvals authorities.

Mr Holmes believes BT maintains its stranglehold on the installation of new equipment on business premises by retaining the right to inspect the work of the independents before final connection.

Mr Richard Woolam, chief executive of the Telecommunications Industry Association, a new trade association with 700 members drawn mainly from the ranks of the new telecommunication companies, said trying to market against BT remained a problem.

Otherwise, early difficulties encountered by the entrepreneurs were similar to those of any small business: Dellfield talks about the shortage of right quality managers; National Telephone Systems struggled to attract cash and marketing expertise; Rocom searched hard for premises.

However, the industry may be entering a new phase, marked by a shake-out of some weaker companies that entered the market seeking quick profits.

Companies doing well at present are likely to spearhead any consolidation over the next few years. Some of them, such as Carphones and National Telephone Systems, have already been gobbling up smaller companies and diversifying. The more adventurous, such as Dellfield and National Telephone Systems, are also pushing into overseas markets.

Many of these companies might have to change their status to continue expanding. Mr Thomas has just sold 15 per cent of Carphone's equity to Telephone Rentals; National Telephone systems is thinking of going to the USM in the next 18 months; Mr Old reckons he will be after a listing in the next couple of years.

David Thomas

Chapter Four

A macroeconomic framework

Much of the controversy between Keynesians and monetarists about the efficacy of demand management policies revolves around the issue of how the supply of national output responds to a change in aggregate demand.

Keynesianism

The emphasis in the 1980s on the supply side of the economy is, in part, a reaction against Keynesian ideas which dominated policy making in the post-war years until the mid 1970s.

According to Keynesians a government can stabilize the national output around its full employment level – the amount produced when the capital stock and labour force are being fully utilized. It can do this by regulating aggregate demand so as to ensure that it equals the amount of output the economy can produce when fully employed. In Keynesian analysis the amount the economy can produce when its productive capacity is fully employed is given; attention is focused on the short-run problems of ensuring that demand is adequate but not excessive, since the latter condition causes inflation and balance of payments deficits. The focus is also on broad aggregates in the economy, rather than on the microeconomic behaviour of individual markets, as Keynesian stabilization policy operates through government manipulation of its own spending and taxation which affects aggregate demand. In Keynesian analysis taxation is an important policy instrument because of its effects on aggregate demand: the disincentive and distortionary effects of taxation are ignored as they are micro-level concerns.

During the period when Keynesian macroeconomic policies were adhered to by British govenments, there were also plenty of government measures directed to the supply side of the economy. These included:

- attempts to plan the economy;
- taking firms into public ownership;
- government-directed investment and industrial restructuring;
- competition policy against restrictive practices and market dominance by firms.

However, most of these policies (with the exception of competition policy) were based on an analysis of market failure, not on a belief in the efficiency of market forces. Furthermore the requirements of demand management predominated, especially during periods of short-run economic crisis when the balance of payments moved into deficit. The predominant view was that the most important objective was to maintain a high level of aggregate demand and that this would ensure both full-capacity working and investment in new capacity.

Monetarism

Keynesian ideas have been increasingly challenged by another school of thought represented as monetarism. Monetarists have little faith in the ability of governments to stabilize real national output by manipulating the level of aggregate demand. They argue that policies designed to increase aggregate demand increase real output only for a couple of years and do so by creating inflation. Once the economy has adjusted to the new rate of inflation, real output falls back to its previous level while the higher rate of inflation persists.

Monetarists therefore advocated the abandonment of Keynesian policies and placed reliance on macroeconomic policies to control inflation. Output and employment are, except for short-run fluctuations, determined by supply side factors which are not amenable to government control using macro-level policy instruments. During the 1960s and 70s the underlying rate of inflation rose, both in Britain and elsewhere, while unemployment increased. A growing perception that Keynesian policies had failed ushered in the adoption of monetarist policies in the UK and elsewhere.

Supply side differences

Keynesian thinking has continued to influence economic commentators and opposition politicians, who have remained critical of monetarism. Much of the controversy between Keynesians and monetarists about the efficacy of demand management policies revolves around the issue of how the supply of national output responds to a change in aggregate demand.

A useful analytical framework for understanding the crucial elements in this controversy is the **aggregate demand** and **aggregate supply** model, the basic elements of which will be explained in this chapter. It will be put to work in Chapter 5, which examines the significance of different ideas about the supply side of the economy for the conduct of macroeconomic policy. The model consists of an aggregate demand function and an aggregate supply function, which together determine real national output and the general price level. The determinants of aggregate demand and aggregate supply will be discussed in turn.

The aggregate demand function

During the 1950s and 60s controversy between Keynesians and monetarists revolved around the determinants of aggregate demand. As the debate matured, a considerable degree of consensus emerged with respect to the determinants of aggregate demand, and the controversy has subsequently centred on the specification of the supply side of a macroeconomic model. It is therefore appropriate to construct an aggregate demand relationship which is common to both Keynesian and monetarist approaches.

Aggregate demand in the model is made up of three major components: consumption, investment and government expenditure.

- *Consumption* depends on disposable incomes – that is, on incomes after tax and social security benefits. It also depends on consumers' wealth, including the amount they hold as money.
- *Investment* depends on firms' expectations about the future pro- fitabililty of investment and upon the cost of investment. This in turn depends upon the rate of interest.
- *Government expenditure* is assumed exogenous – that is, deter- mined solely by the government at its own discretion.

In order to keep the model simple it will be restricted here to a closed economy. (In an open economy exports are added to and imports subtracted from aggregate demand.)

Changes in the price level affect both consumption and investment. Firstly, consumption is affected because it depends on wealth. The value of some assets rises when the price level falls. The real value of a given nominal amount of money (£100 for example) rises if the price level falls because the money can now buy more goods. So if the price level falls the real quantity of money held increases, consumers are wealthier and therefore demand more goods and services. This is often referred to as the **Pigou effect**.

Secondly, investment is affected by a change in the price level, again because a fall in the price level increases the real quantity of money that people hold. This increase in the real money supply lowers interest rates, and a fall in interest rates stimulates investment.

Given the above behaviour of consumption and investment, a *fall* in the price level *increases* aggregate demand via its effect in increasing the *real* quantity of money, given that the *nominal* quantity of money

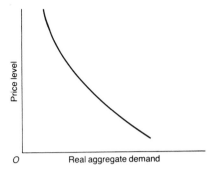

Figure 10   The aggregate demand function

remains unchanged. A *rise* in the price level *reduces* aggregate demand.

The aggregate demand function is, then, the relationship between the amount of aggregate demand and the price level. The lower the price level, the higher is the amount of aggregate demand in the economy, all other things remaining unchanged. An aggregate demand function is shown in Figure 10.

The aggregate supply function

To complete the model the aggregate supply function is needed since this indicates how firms in the economy respond to changes in aggregate demand. As the aggregate demand and supply (AD/AS) model is used for short-run analysis, the economy's productive capacity is assumed fixed. The aggregate supply function depicts how, with capacity fixed, firms change their supply of output in response to changes in aggregate demand. Thinking back to the production function in Chapter 2, the fixed capacity assumption implies the following assumptions:

1. The capital stock is constant.
2. The current state of technical knowledge is unchanged as there is no technical progress.
3. The size of the labour force is unchanged (i.e. the number of people of working age is constant and those factors which determine people's supply of working hours – such as taxation, social security or trade union restrictive practices – remain unchanged).
4. The productivity of labour is constant. Hence there is no increase in, for example, the skills of the labour force or in the efficiency of working practices.

Given that firms' productive capacity is fixed, what will induce them to increase the amount of real output they are willing to supply?

- Is an increase in demand by customers sufficient?
- Or do producers also require an increase in the price of output?
- Or are firms unwilling to produce any more at all with their existing capacity because it is fully utilized?

The answers to these questions are determined by the nature of the supply function. At the level of the whole economy the aggregate supply function is the relationship between the average price level and the amount of real national output domestic firms are willing to supply, given that the productive capacity of the economy and the prices of factors of production (including wages) remain unchanged.

Figure 11 shows three possible shapes for the aggregate supply function, which we can analyse as follows:

(a) If the aggregate supply function is *perfectly elastic*, as is AC, then firms are prepared to expand production at the existing price level.
(b) If the aggregate supply curve is *perfectly inelastic*, as is DF, then firms are willing to supply OF output whatever the price level. OF is the amount of output the economy can produce when its existing productive capacity is fully utilized.
(c) If the aggregate supply function is upward sloping up to full capacity, and is given by a curved line such as BD, firms will supply more output so long as the price level increases.

Whether the aggregate supply function is an inverted-L shape (like ACD), or upward-sloping (like BD) or vertical (like FD) depends on how firms' **marginal costs** behave as their output increases. Marginal costs could be constant, rising, or – in the full-capacity case – tend to be infinitely large.

Marginal costs, in turn, depend on two factors. One is the **marginal productivity of labour,** assuming labour to be the variable factor of production, with capital held constant. The other is the cost of employing labour, which is made up of the wage rate and non-wage costs such as welfare payments (pension contribution and National Insurance). The marginal cost of an additional unit of output produced by employing one more unit of labour is given by the following relationship:

$$\text{Marginal cost} = \frac{\text{Wage rate} + \text{non-wage labour costs}}{\text{Marginal product of labour}}$$

You can check that you understand this relationship by trying out a

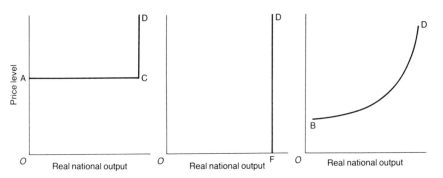

Figure 11 Three possible shapes for the aggregate supply function

few numerical examples. For instance, if employing one extra hour of labour costs the firm £8 and the marginal product of that labour is 16 units of output, then the marginal cost per unit output is 50p.

Let us now look in turn at the three cases depicted in Figure 11. In each case the wage rage is held constant, so that the behaviour of marginal costs depends on what happens to the marginal product of labour.

An inverted L-shaped marginal curve
This is the standard case which Keynesian economists argue holds in a recession when firms are under-utilizing their existing productive capacity. Some of the capital stock is standing idle and is not being manned. Additional output can be produced by hiring more labour to run the idle machines, and so the marginal product of labour is constant as output is increased. Furthermore, if firms are reluctant to dismiss their workforce in a recession – even if there is not enough for them to do – the marginal product of labour would rise at first when output is expanded from a low level of capacity utilization. A constant marginal product of labour means constant marginal costs and so a perfectly elastic aggregate supply function with respect to the price level.

An upwards-sloping marginal cost curve
Alternatively firms' marginal cost curves could be upward-sloping for either of two reasons:

- As more labour is put to work with a fixed amount of capital equipment, the marginal product of the variable factor (labour) declines. This is the usual case of declining marginal returns.
- Firms have plants built at different times, embodying different technologies. Some plants (usually the older ones) operate at higher

costs than others. The high-cost plants are closed during a recession. As the economy moves out of recession and output expands, the high-cost plants are put back into operation. Hence marginal costs *rise* as output expands. Now, if marginal costs rise as output increases, firms are only willing to produce more output if they can get a higher price for it. In this case the aggregate supply function is upward-sloping.

Full capacity
At the limit full capacity occurs when it is physically impossible to increase output further. This is the usual meaning of the term in a basic Keynesian model.

However, full capacity can also refer to the quantity of output per period of time that the capital equipment was designed to produce when operating at *minimum average cost*. This is referred to as **designed full capacity.** A firm can expand beyond its designed full capacity by various means (such as running its plant for an extra shift a day), but this will raise marginal costs because of extra maintenance, say. The more output is expanded beyond its designed full capacity level, the higher will be marginal costs – until eventually the marginal cost curve becomes vertical. At this point the short-run aggregate supply function is also vertical.

Keynesian and monetarist aggregate supply functions
Keynesian models assume either an inverted-L or upward-sloping aggregated supply function which becomes vertical at full capacity. Many Keynesians hold that the aggregate supply function has horizontal, upward-sloping and vertical sections, depending on the extent of capacity utilization.

Monetarists, on the other hand, distinguish between an upward-sloping short-run aggregate supply function and a long-run aggregate supply function. Whereas the latter is vertical at designed full capacity, in the short-run firms will produce in excess of designed full capacity if prices are high enough to make this seem profitable.

The Keynesian and monetarist specifications of the aggregate supply function are shown in Figures 12 and 13 respectively.

Shifts in the aggregate supply function
The short-run horizontal or upward-sloping aggregate supply function will shift *if there is a change in the money wage rate*. If there is an increase in the money wage rate – due, for instance, to trade union pressure – then the short-run aggregate supply function will shift

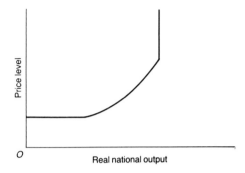

Figure 12 A Keynesian aggregate supply function

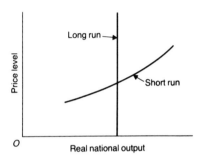

Figure 13 A monetararist aggregate supply function

upwards. It will also shift to the left if it is upward-sloping. This happens because a rise in the money wage rate increases firms' marginal costs, so firms are now willing to supply a given quantity of output only if they get a higher price for it. The effect of an increase in the money wage rate is shown in Figures 14 and 15 for the Keynesian and monetarist cases respectively.

The long-run aggregate supply curve (or the vertical section of the Keynesian AS curve) will shift to the right *if there are any changes in the economy which increase its productive capacity.* Such changes might include

- investment, which increases the capital stock;
- an increase in the labour force, which may occur because

(a) the population of working age increases, or
(b) a higher proportion of the population of working age seeks employment because the returns from working become relatively more attractive (this could occur if income tax rates are cut or if unemployment benefit falls);

- an increase in the productivity of capital or labour due to technical progress or to improved working practices which increase efficiency.

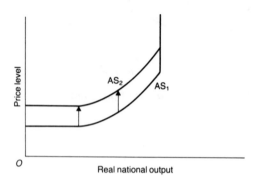

Figure 14 The effect of an increase in the money wage rate on the Keynesian AS function

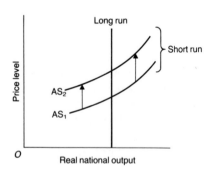

Figure 15 The effect of an increase in the money wage rate on a monetarist short–run AS function

KEY WORDS	
Keynesianism	Marginal costs
Monetarism	Marginal productivity
Aggregate demand	of labour
Aggregate supply	Designed full capacity
Pigou effect	

Reading list

Brown, C.V., 'Supply side economics,' *Sterling Economics Teaching Papers*, University of Sterling and the Economics Association, 1985.

Brown, C.V., *Unemployment and inflation: an Introduction to Macroeconomics*, Basil Blackwell, 1984.

Levačić, R., 'The analysis of economic management: the aggregate demand and aggregate supply model', in Thompson G., Brown, V. and Levačić, R. (eds), *Managing the UK Economy*, Polity Press, 1987.

ESSAY TOPICS

1. Examine the arguments for and against a significant increase in public expenditure.
   University of London Schools Examinations Board, June 1986.
2. Discuss the factors which determine a country's aggregate supply function, distinguishing between
   (a) those that determine designed full capacity, and
   (b) those that determine the elasticity of the aggregate supply function with respect to changes in the price level.
3. How would you expect the tax changes introduced in recent UK budgets to affect the quantity of investment undertaken and its allocation?
4. What problems are there in determining whether an economy is operating at 'full capacity'?

Data response question 5

The effects of policy measures

The extracts below are summaries of measures introduced by the government or proposed by the Labour opposition. Explain what effects, if any, you would expect *each* of the policy measures to have on:

1. the demand for labour by firms;
2. the supply of labour;
3. the size and efficiency of the capital stock;
4. the productivity of the labour force;

and hence explain what is the intended effect on the long-run aggregate supply function.

What effects would you expect B and C below to have on the aggregate demand curve?

Extract A

'The other main tax proposals (of the 1986 Budget) are:

- a halving of the stamp duty on share transactions, from 1 per cent to ½ per cent financed by a broadening of the tax base;
- abolition of capital transfer tax on lifetime gifts by individuals;
- indefinite extension of the Business Expansion Scheme.

   (*Economic Progress Report,* No.183, March/April 1986)

Extract B

'The government believes that people should be left free to spend or save more of their own money – that lower tax economies work better than higher tax economies. The Budget therefore gives priority to reducing income tax.

'The basic rate comes down by 2p in the pound. This brings it down to 27 per cent compared with 33 per cent in 1978–79 and a peak of 35 per cent in 1975–76 to 1976–77.'

(*Economic Progress Report,* No. 189, March/April 1987)

Extract C

'The national insurance surcharge, paid by employers on everyone working for them, was abolished in 1984.

'The system of National Insurance contributions was restructured in 1985. Lower rates of employers' and employees' contributions were introduced for the lower paid, financed in part by removing the upper limit on employers' contributions for the higher paid. This made it cheaper for employers to take on lower-paid workers and allowed those workers to keep more of what they earned.'

(*Economic Progress Report*, No.192, October 1987)

Extract D

'For modern, wealth-creating industry we need a well-trained work-force. British industry now carries out less than half of the training of our main competitors. Labour will therefore establish a national training programme to bring about a major advance in the spread and standard of skills.

'For young people we will establish an integrated, high-quality Foundation Programme that will guarantee for all 16-year olds at least two years' of education, training and work experience according to their needs.

'The Adult Skillplan will develop lifelong training and education for everyone needing to supplement and update skills in work, with particular emphasis given to training for women.'

(*Britain will Win*, Labour manifesto, June 1987)

Chapter Five

Keynesian and monetarist policies

How long increases in real output and employment last following a boost to aggregate demand depends in monetarist analysis, on the time it takes money wages to adjust to rising goods prices.

═══

The controversy between Keynesians and monetarists over appropriate macroeconomic policies stems very largely from their different views on how the supply side of the economy responds to changes in aggregate demand, as we saw in Chapter 4. To see this more clearly let us take the three shapes of the aggregate supply function shown in Figure 11.

The inverted-L aggregate supply curve
In this basic version of the Keynesian model of the economy, the level of aggregate demand determines the level of real national output up to full employment. So long as output is in perfectly elastic supply, any increase in demand calls forth an equivalent increase in the supply of output. This is shown in the top half of Figure 16, where the upward shift in the aggregate demand function – which the government could engineer by increasing its expenditure or by lowering taxes – expands output from Y_1 to Y_2. The price level remains unchanged.

This analysis is identical to that found in most A-level textbooks using the Keynesian cross or 45° diagram. These books do not usually make explicit that the model depends on the assumption of an inverted-L aggregate supply function. The Keynesian cross diagram is inserted in the bottom half of Figure 16 to show the correspondence between this approach and that of the AD/AS model. The shift in the expenditure function from AB to CD is equivalent to the shift in the aggregate demand function from AD_1 to AD_2. The intersection of the expenditure function with the 45° line shows the level of national income at which the goods market is in equilibrium. This is because at this level of national income the amount of output demanded is the same as the level of national income. *This intersection does not show the equilibrium between the demand and supply of national output.* For levels of output Y_1 and Y_2 in the lower half of Figure 16 to be equilibrium quantities *supplied,* one has to assume that the supply of national output is perfectly elastic, as shown in the top half of the figure. With this assumption, what is demanded is automatically supplied.

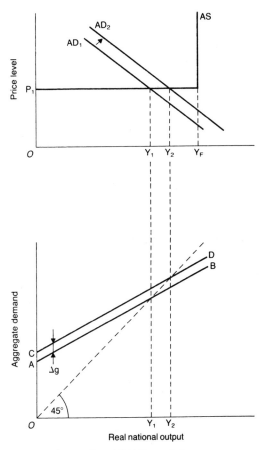

Figure 16 A basic Keynesian AD/AS model

An upward-sloping aggregate supply function

The basic Keynesian model assumes a constant price level and so is not particularly useful for analysing an economy in which rising aggregate demand contributes to inflation at most times, and not just when the economy is deemed to be fully employed. A model with an upward-sloping aggregate supply function does predict that an increase in aggregate demand will cause a rise in the price level as well as in real output. This is shown in Figure 17.

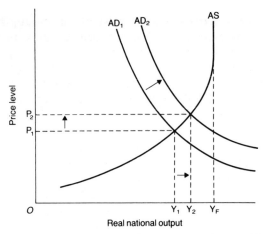

Figure 17 The effect of an increase in aggregate demand in a Keynesian model with an upward-sloping aggregate supply function

Aggregate demand is increased by the government spending more, taxing less or expanding the money supply. In Figure 17 the consequence of such an expansionary policy is shown as a shift in the aggregate demand curve from AD_1 to AD_2. The outcome is an increase in real output from Y_1 to Y_2 and a rise in the price level from P_1 to P_2. Firms are willing to increase the supply of output but only if prices rise so that a profit can be made on the extra units of output. The aggregate supply function slopes upward, as explained in Chapter 4, because the marginal product of labour declines as output is expanded. This causes firms' marginal costs to rise even though the wage paid to labour is unchanged. The Keynesian model assumes that the money wage rate remains unchanged when demand is expanded because there is **involuntary unemployment**. This means that the unemployed are willing to work at the going **money wage rate** even though the price level rises to cause the **real wage rate** (the money wage deflated by the price level) to decline.

The monetarist analysis of changes in aggregate demand

The monetarist critique of the Keynesian analysis of **demand management** focuses on the Keynesian assumption of involuntary unemployment.

In a monetarist model there is no pool of unemployed willing to work at or below the current real wage rate. If goods prices rise in response to an increase in demand, then workers will seek a commensurate rise in their money wage rate in order to preserve their real wage.

The response to an increase in aggregate demand in a monetarist AD/AS model is shown in Figure 18. The initial level of national output is Y_1 and the price level is P_1 given by the intersection of aggregate demand curve AD_1 with the aggregate supply curve AS_1. The government seeks to lower unemployment by increasing aggregate demand to AD_2. Initially the money wage stays put at its original level of W_1, so the economy moves up aggregate supply curve AS_1. Firms raise prices, the real wage falls and so firms demand more labour. At first workers do not realize that prices are rising; firms start offering slightly higher wages to attract labour. Workers mistakenly think they are being offered higher real wages because they do not realize that the general price level will rise. Consequently more labour is supplied to firms. Output rises and unemployment falls.

But after a while, as workers realize that inflation is occurring and that real wages have fallen, they start to reduce their supply of working hours and to seek higher money wages. As the money wage rate rises so the AS curve in Figure 18 shifts up to the left. Eventually, when the rise in money wages catches up with the rise in the price level, the real wage is back to its original value. The aggregate supply function in Figure 18 has shifted up to AS_2. The aggregate demand curve AD_2 and the aggregate supply curve AS_2 intersect at the original level of real output, Y_1. The price level, however, is now higher at P_3.

In a monetarist AD/AS model the upward-sloping aggregate supply function is a short-run relationship. It shifts in response to changes in

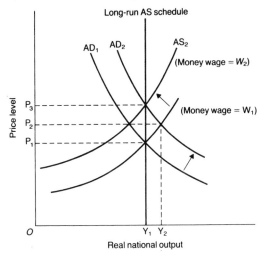

Figure 18 A monetarist model: the temporary effect on real output of an increase in aggregate demand

the money wage rate, while the money wage itself rises in response to increased goods prices which are brought about by rising aggregate demand. Increased aggregate demand can only bring about a *temporary* increase in real output. This increase lasts only so long as prices are rising more rapidly than money wages so that the real wage is brought down by inflation. Because of the lower real wage firms demand more labour. But once money wages have fully adjusted for inflation, output and employment return to their original level which is determined by the underlying productive capacity of the economy.

The productive capacity of the economy cannot be increased by raising the price level. This is why the long-run aggregate supply function in a monetarist model is shown as a vertical line in the AD/AS diagram, as it is in Figure 18. In the long-run, real output is perfectly inelastic with respect to the price level. Here the long-run refers to the period over which money wages adjust fully to changes in the price level. In the short-run, money wages adjust with a lag to changes in the price level. It is this **lagged adjustment** of wages to changes in prices that produces an upwards-sloping short-run aggregate supply function. For a given productive capacity – that is, for a given long-run aggregate supply function – there is a family of short-run aggregate supply functions. The position of each one depends on the current money wage rate. The position of the economy on the current short-run aggregate supply function is determined by the amount of aggregate demand measured at the current price level.

Expectations about inflation

How long increases in real output and employment last following a boost to aggregate demand depends, in monetarist analysis, on the time it takes money wages to adjust to rising goods prices. The more slowly money wages adjust to inflation, the longer the increase in real output persists. An important factor in determining the speed with which money wages adjust is workers' **expectations** about inflation.

If people are backward-looking then they base their expectations of a variable entirely on the past values of that variable. So expectations about future inflation depend on past rates of inflation. This means that when inflation is accelerating expectations of inflation always lag behind actual inflation. If money wage rises are based on expected inflation then they always lag behind actual inflation. The more slowly inflationary expectations adjust, the longer it takes the short-run aggregate supply function in Figure 18 to shift up to the left; and so the rise in real output lasts longer.

Backward-looking expectations are not *rational* if they are persistently incorrect because of the failure to use available information in order to make better predictions of future inflation. If, for example, inflation is explained by changes in the money supply and/or the exchange rate, then it would be rational to base expectations about future inflation upon past and current values of the rate of growth of the money supply and changes in the exchange rate.

Rational expectations are defined as expectations which are based on all the available relevant information and which consequently are not systematically and persistently mistaken. The assumption of rational expectations began to be applied by economists in the late 1970s, particularly by a group known as the **New Classical School** of macroeconomics. Introduced into a monetarist AD/AS model to explain the adjustment of money wages, rational expectations can give rise to the prediction that government policies to expand aggregate demand do not even have a temporary effect in increasing real output.

This is because economic agents immediately predict the inflation that will result from expansionary government policies. Money wages rise at the same rate as inflation, so there is no decline in the real wage rate. In terms of Figure 18, the aggregate supply function shifts up instantaneously from AS_1 to AS_2 and so there is no increase in real output.

The role of money wages

The construction of the AD/AS model draws attention to the crucial role of wages in determining output, both in the long-run and in the short-run. In the long-run it is the real wage rate that matters, since this affects the amount of labour that is supplied and demanded. In short-run adjustments the money wage is also important. Government attempts to increase output and employment by raising aggregate demand are likely to be thwarted if money wages rise too fast.

Throughout the post-war period the UK economy has tended to experience greater upward pressures on money wages than comparable economies. As Figure 19 shows (based on NEDO data), of the major industrialized economies only Italy has experienced higher wage inflation. In the 1950s and 60s this was seen primarily as a cause of **cost push inflation.** By the late 1970s, however, more attention was being given to the difficulties wage pushfulness posed for government attempts to run the economy at full employment without generating accelerating inflation.

Policies aimed at reducing the rate of increase of money wages, by operating on the supply side of the labour market, are not new to the

1980s. **Incomes policies,** whereby the government legislates against wage increases above a certain norm or negotiates voluntary restraint with business and union leaders, were intermittently practised from 1961 to 1979. Policies to reform wage bargaining have also been debated for several decades. In terms of the AD/AS model these policies aim to slow down, or prevent, the upwards drift of the AS function.

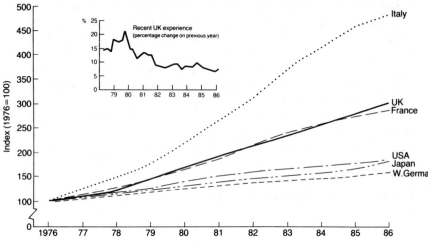

Figure 19 Wages per head in manufacturing

KEY WORDS

Involuntary unemployment	Expectations
Money wage rate	Rational expectations
Real wage rate	New Classical School
Demand management	Cost push inflation
Lagged adjustment	Incomes policies

Reading list

Levačić, R., 'The analysis of economic management: the aggregate demand and aggregate supply model', in Thompson, G., Brown, V. and Levačić, R. (eds), *Managing the UK Economy,* Polity Press, 1987.

Pennant-Rea and Crook, 'Expecting the future', in *The Economist Economics,* Penguin, 1986

Shaw, G.K., *Rational Expectations: an Explanatory Exposition,* Wheatsheaf, 1984.

Essay topics

1. How do Keynesian and monetarist analyses of the effects of an increase in aggregate demand on real national output differ?

2. 'In the Keynesian view governments should regulate real national output by manipulating aggregate demand. According to supply side economists the role of macroeconomic policy is to maintain a stable price level.' Explain how these different policy recommendations are derived using the aggregate demand and supply model.

3. Use the aggregate demand and supply model to show the differences between Keynesian and supply side analyses of the effects of a reduction in income tax on real national output.

4. Discuss the role of expectations about inflation in determining the extent to which a government induced expansion in aggregate demand will increase real national output.

5. Examine Samuel Britan's view that 'governments cannot spend their way into target levels of employment'.
Oxford and Cambridge Schools Examination Board, June 1986.

Data response question 6

Teaching rational expectations at A-level

Read the accompanying extract from Beachill, B., *Economics*, No.99, autumn 1987, and study the price and wage inflation graphs.

1. Undertake the same analysis as Beachill does with the augmented Phillips curve but using the AD/AS model in which there is a change in the price level rather than in the rate of inflation.

2. What assumption about the long-run aggregate supply curve is equivalent to a vertical long-run Phillips curve?

3. From the graphical data on the rate of price and wage inflation in the UK, assess the hypothesis that changes in money wages are due entirely to rational expectations about inflation. The wage graph shows manual wages for all industries and services.

The concept of rational expectations (RE)

Agents have RE if they, on averge, *correctly* forecast the future values of relevant economic variables; i.e. people, on average, guess right. To be more formal and specific, RE assumes all agents:

1. make use of ALL the currently available information they can obtain. This *may* include (as is often assumed) knowledge about (a) the underlying structure of the economy or particular economic institution (i.e. the 'model'), and (b) present and future anticipated government policy; as well as data on the current and past values of relevant variables.

2. do not make *continual*, systematic errors in their forecasts. Learning is immediate and forecasting mistakes are therefore purely random errors arising from uncertainty (unanticipated shocks). Without uncertainty, RE becomes perfect foresight – no forecast errors are made at all.

3. are essentially forward-looking rather than backward-looking. Agents do not form expectations/forecasts by simply and naïvely extrapolating past trends in the data. This assumption is implied by the first two. Say for example that inflation has been on a slowly rising trend in the last few years but then there is a sudden and dramatic fall in the price of oil. Rational agents will not expect inflation to continue on its present trend but will use this new information (this piece of 'news') to form a more accurate forecast of future inflation.

The augmented Phillips curve

In the conventional explanation of the shifting Phillips curve (PC) expectations are again assumed to be static or backward-looking. Short-run movements along the PC (e.g. from A to B) giving a reduction in unemployment below the natural rate U_N are possible because

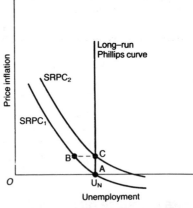

workers' expectations of future inflation lag behind reality. Expectations, however, eventually catch up with reality and unemployment goes back to its natural level (at point C). The PC is vertical in the *long-run*. Keeping unemployment below the natural rate therefore requires accelerating inflation (created and validated by accelerating monetary growth) so that expectations continually lag behind reality. At the natural rate inflation and expectations are constant and equal. The short-run PC therefore shifts outwards over time because of increased inflationary expectations.

Again this explanation relies on seemingly rather naïve behaviour – workers consistently *under-predict* (or over-predict in the case of disinflationary policies) actual inflation and hence take jobs (because they mistakenly assume real wages have risen) which they later quit. Surely this systematic miscalculation wouldn't continue? Workers would quickly see that say 10% monetary growth leads ultimately to 10% inflation with **no** change in real wages and would therefore **not** mistakenly take up extra jobs. This is precisely the implication of assuming RE.

With RE, workers **correctly** anticipate inflation (except, again, for random forecasting errors due to uncertainty/ unanticipated shocks) and therefore do NOT mistakenly take jobs. **No** short-run reduction of unemployment below the natural rate occurs – the PC is vertical in the *short-run as well*. In terms of the diagram the economy moves from A to C immediately. Assuming RE has produced a startling result – the *policy ineffectiveness proposition* of the New Classical Macroeconomics. (N.B. This result required RE *and* continuous market clearing in the labour market, i.e. perfectly flexible wages. If wages are inflexible to some degree than government stabilisation policy can still be effective even given RE on the part of workers.)

B.Beachill

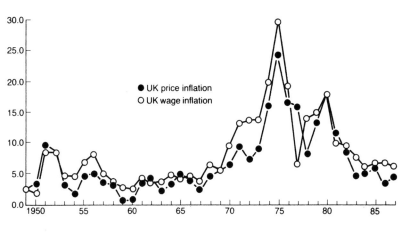

Chapter Six

Labour market policies

*In having these aims for labour market policies, the Thatcher
governments have not differed from previous governments. The
difference has lain in the types of policy adopted.*

The government's labour market policies are micro-level policies.
They are being considered here after the AD/AS model so that you can
see how such policies fit into the macroeconomic analysis of the
economy. Labour market policies contribute to higher real national
output if they succeed in

- increasing labour productivity
  and/or
- reducing the cost of labour to employers.

Any permanent reduction in labour unit costs will shift the long-run
aggregate supply function out to the right.

In having these aims for labour market policies, the Thatcher
governments have not differed from previous governments. The
difference has lain in the types of policy adopted which, in turn, stem
from the supply side analysis of the workings of the economy outlined
in Chapter 3. This has led to a rejection of prices and incomes policies
since they distort the operation of the price mechanism. The main
problem with the labour market diagnosed by supply-siders is its
inability to adjust flexibility in response to changes in the conditions of
demand and supply.

Trade unions

One major reason for this inflexibility, according to the supply-siders,
is trade unions since they are monopolistic sellers of labour. Excessive
trade union power is held responsible for holding down labour
productivity by maintaining restrictive practices and for raising real
wages above competitive market levels.

In line with these views, the Conservative government has changed
the laws regulating trade unions in order to reduce their bargaining
power and to require union leaders to consult their membership more.
The law now requires a vote of at least 80 per cent of the membership

before a closed shop can be created. The 1982 Employment Act extended similar voting rules to permit existing closed shops to continue. A particularly effective measure has been to define a trade dispute narrowly to cover only the immediate employer and its employees. Only a strike which has been approved by a majority of the union's members in a secret ballot is immune from civil action for damages. The 1980 Employment Act also removed unions' immunity from civil legal action against secondary picketing. Unions have become liable to successful court action for damages by parties adversely affected by industrial action which no longer has legal immunity. In addition the selective dismissal of strikers who disobey a legal injunction is now possible without financial loss on the part of the employer.

Reducing labour costs

Various measures have aimed to reduce labour costs. For example, the scope of **minimum wage laws** operated by Wages Councils for specific industries has been reduced. The number of industries covered has been cut and the regulations restricted to adults.

Firms' employment costs have been cut by abolishing the National Insurance surcharge which firms had to pay for each employee. The relative cost of employing low-paid labour was reduced by introducing a lower rate of National Insurance contributions for those on low wages.

Social security payments to the unemployed have been cut or made more difficult to obtain in order to increase the willingness of workers to work for lower wages. In 1980 the earnings-related element of unemployment benefit was abolished. In 1987 unemployed 16- and 17-year-olds became ineligible for benefit if they refused a place on the Youth Training Scheme.

Increasing labour mobility

A favourite government phrase is 'improving the flexibility of the labour market'. This includes making it easier for people to change jobs. Personal pension schemes have been made more attractive through tax relief; this is intended to eliminate the cost of job mobility due to loss of pension rights in a company pension scheme.

One of the major obstacles to job mobility from the northern regions of high unemployment to the prosperous south-east is the much higher cost of private housing there and the difficulty of obtaining council housing in a new area. However, the setting up of a Tenants' Exchange Scheme and a National Mobility Office are small beer compared with the problems of escalating house prices in the south-east, cuts in local authority housing programmes and the continued absence of a significant private rented sector.

Training and education

There is much criticism of the poor quality of the labour force in Britain compared with Japan, West Germany and other industrialized countries, this being attributed mainly to an inadequate education and training system. This diagnosis has widespread support, including by all the major political parties. Given the government's beliefs in the efficiency of markets, its preference is for considerable private sector involvement in training. In fact one of its early moves was to abolish many of the industrial training boards set up by a Labour government in the 1960s and financed by compulsory levies.

The Training Commission (the renamed Manpower Services Commission) has been used as a major agent for instituting training programmes in conjunction with the private sector. The Youth Training Scheme, which offers every 16/17-year-old a two-year programme of work-related training and education, is one of its major initiatives. However, it has been criticized for doing little to increase the supply of skilled workers in the skill-shortage areas or to make up for the decline in apprenticeships.

The Training Commission also provides retraining schemes for the unemployed. In February 1988 a White Paper, *Training for Employment,* announced a new £1.4 billion training scheme which aims to provide 600 000 places a year for all those aged 18 to 24 who have been unemployed for longer than six months. All trainees are to be paid £10–12 a week in addition to their current benefits.

A further initiative is the Open College, providing coordinated programmes of vocational training using television and distance teaching methods, as well as locally based courses.

The key problem in devising efficient training programmes is that government agencies are less well placed than firms to gather information on the changing skill patterns required in a dynamic economy; but firms are reluctant to undertake the cost of training employees who may well leave and take their expensively acquired skills elsewhere.

Labour market policies illustrate well the point that an increased emphasis on the importance of the supply side of the economy is not confined to market-oriented economists or to conservative/right-wing governments. It is characteristic of a broad spectrum of economic and political thinking in the 1980s throughout the world. Keynesians, too, have modified their preoccupation with aggregate demand and now give much more emphasis to the workings of labour markets and to the role of the capital stock in determining the supply of output.

KEY WORDS	
Minimum wage laws	Training
Labour mobility	Training Commission

Reading list

Ireland, N., 'Profit-sharing to promote employment', *Economic Review*, May 1987.

Shields, J., 'Job creation and labour market policy', *Economic Review*, September 1987.

Essay topics

1. 'Trade unions should currently be striving to keep wage increases as small as possible.' Discuss.
   Oxford and Cambridge Schools Examination Board, June 1986

2. 'In order to reduce unemployment Keynesians advocate macro-economic policies whereas supply side economists recommend microeconomic policies'. Discuss.

3. In what ways would you expect profit related pay schemes to increase the economy's capacity to supply output?

4. Discuss what policies governments can pursue in order to raise labour productivity.

Data response question 7

Profit-related pay

The extract below is taken from an *Economic Progress Report* supplement on the 1987 Budget. Read the extract and answer the following questions.

1. If profit-related pay were successful what would its effect be on
   (a) the long-run aggregate supply function
   (b) the short-run aggregate supply function?

2. Use an AD/AS model to analyse how these changes would affect real output and the price level.

3. How might PRP act to reduce unemployment below what it might otherwise be in response to a fall in aggregate demand?

The 1987 Budget comment

After consultations following the last Budget, the government has decided to introduce a new relief against income tax to encourage the spread of profit-related pay (PRP). This is intended to promote greater flexibility in the labour market.

The government sees two main advantages in PRP:

- it gives employees a direct stake – and so a personal interest – in the success of the business for which they work;
- it enables pay to respond more flexibly to changing market conditions – and the more flexible is pay, the more secure are jobs.

The essence of the scheme in the Budget is that, on certain conditions, half of all PRP payments in the private sector will be entirely free of tax. The maximum amount of PRP eligible for tax relief will be £3000 a year or 20 per cent of an employee's total pay, whichever is the lower. So for a married man on average earnings:

- if 5 per cent of pay is profit-related, the tax relief will be worth about £1.50 a week, equivalent to a penny off the basic rate;
- if 20 per cent of pay is profit-related, the tax relief could be worth about £6.00 a week, equivalent to 4p off the basic rate.

Chapter Seven

Perspectives on supply side economics

A consensus view is beginning to emerge that both demand management and supply side policies are required.

The term **supply side economics** must be distinguished from an emphasis on the importance of **supply side factors** in determining a country's economic performance. The latter are widely accepted and have been given considerably more emphasis in policy making in the 1980s. However, the economic *analysis* of the functioning and role of markets, from which supply side economic policies are derived, is far more contentious.

There are many economists, politicians and others – often of a socialist persuasion – who reject the supply side reliance on markets and cite many instances of alleged **market failure.** In particular, Britain's poor economic performance in the post-war decades is attributed to lack of investment in the British economy by the financial institutions, and a failure by British management to undertake sufficient research and development in the fields of new technology, or to train adequately. Active government intervention is advocated as the appropriate solution, whereby the government both provides funds for investment, R and D and training, and decides how to allocate these funds. Some examples of such policy advocacy are given in the data response question at the end of this chapter.

Another area of disagreement is the role of **demand management.** The orthodox monetarist (and new classical) position is that the government should maintain a low and stable budget deficit – ideally a **balanced budget** – and operate monetary policy so as to keep inflation in check. The purpose of macroeconomic policy in this view is to maintain a stable economic environment and to leave the supply side decisions about employment, investment and production to firms operating in competitive markets. In contrast, the Keynesian view is still that there is an important role for government in managing demand so as to offset the instability inherent in private sector adjustment.

A consensus view is beginning to emerge that both demand management and supply side policies are required. The large increase in unemployment that accompanied the 1979–81 deflationary fiscal and monetary policies (which were used to reduce inflation, from the higher teens to the 3–5 per cent range) confirmed the judgement that the labour market does not, in the UK at least, adjust smoothly to such changes – as was predicted by applying the new classical theory of rational expectations. The government is now operating more relaxed **fiscal and monetary policies.** It is increasing its spending and reducing taxation (though still justifying the latter on supply side grounds), and has ceased to operate a tight monetary policy.

Overview and conclusions

As this review of supply side economic policies shows, they encompass a wide range of measures, many of them applying at the micro-level to particular sectors and markets. They are derived from an analysis of the efficiency of the competitive market as an instrument for economic progress and the enhancement of **social welfare.**

In a macroeconomic framework, supply side policies aim to enlarge the productive capacity of the economy by increasing the quantity and quality of the capital stock and the labour force and by improving the efficiency with which they are put to work. Supply side policies are mainly analysed as aimed at shifting the aggregate supply function to the right in the long-run. A subsidiary aim of supply side policies is to improve the response of aggregate supply to changes in aggregate demand, so that reductions in aggregate demand lead to less unemployment and increases in aggregate demand cause less inflation.

Empirical assessment of the success of supply side policies is inevitably contentious and involves balanced judgement. At the macro-level there is now clear evidence of improved performance in the UK economy in terms of increased productivity and growth; but this may be only temporary and unemployment remains high, though declining since 1986. To what extent this is because of supply side policies (including better incentives from lower income tax rates) and to what extent it is due to an old-fashioned Keynesian **reflation** (from tax cuts and increased government spending) is currently the subject of both academic and political debate. At the micro-level, assessment of supply side policies requires investigation of their effects in individual markets where they have been applied – to telecommunications, buses, pensions and financial markets, to name but a few. The effects on different sectors – on small businesses, on manufacturing investment, on personal share holding, on the incentives to work and on wage determination – are also being assessed.

The micro and macroeconomic framework provided in this booklet should help you to relate the quite disparate topics you learn about from a variety of sources to the supply side analysis of the economy. As supply side economics and supply side policies cover such a wide range of topics you will also be able to discover more about them in the other booklets in this series.

KEY WORDS

Supply side economics	Balanced budget
Supply side factors	Fiscal and monetary policies
Market failure	Social welfare
Demand management	Reflation

Reading list

Lord Aldington, 'Britain's manufacturing industry', *Royal Bank of Scotland Review*, No. 151, September 1986.

Budd, A., 'Conservative economic policy', *Economic Review*, September 1987.

Levačić, R., 'Supply side economics', in Atkinson, G.B. (ed), *Developments in Economics*, Vol. 1, Causeway Press, 1985.

Oxford Review of Economic Policy, vol. 4, No.1, Spring 1988, 'Long-run economic performance in the UK'

Essay topics

1. We have gone very far in the past 50 years in expanding the role of government in the economy. That intervention has been costly in economic terms? (Milton Friedman, *Free to Choose*)
   'Strong and effective guidance of the economy by the government will ensure good performance.' (J.K. Galbraith, *Economics and the Art of Controversy*).
   Outline the basis for each of these views and, in the light of British experience, say which you think is justified.
   Joint Matriculation Board, June 1985

2. 'It is generally accepted that supply side factors are crucial determinants of a country's economic performance, but supply side economic policies are much more contentious.' Discuss.

3. How do the opposition parties' supply side policies with respect to taxation, the labour market and industry differ from those of the Thatcher government?
4. Explain how different views regarding the efficiency of markets lead to recommendations of distinctly different government policies towards industry.

Data response question 8

'Alternative supply side policies'

Read the accompanying extracts from the Labour and Alliance parties' 1987 General Election manifestos, and answer the following questions.

1. How did the Labour and SDP–Liberal Alliance supply side proposals differ from those of the Conservative government with respect to investment, taxation and the labour supply?
2. Relate these policy differences to different views regarding the efficiency of markets and governments in allocating resources.

Labour: New strength for industry

For eight years British industry has been left to drift and decline. Our oil revenues have been wasted and the City has concentrated upon short-term movements of capital at the expense of British manufacturing industry. The huge capital outflow of £110 billion since 1979 is ruinous evidence of the Tories' lack of concern for the strength of the British economy.

Labour is committed to rebuilding our industrial base. Our country must make the best use of computers and information technology to develop the modern means of making a living as the oil runs down and the pressures of technical change and international competition intensify.

We will:

- Establish a capital repatriation scheme using the tax system to attract and retain British savings and investment in Britain.

- Set up the British Industrial Investment Bank, with strong bases in Scotland, Wales and English regions, to ensure finance for industry where it is needed, when it is needed and on terms which encourage long term development.

- Implement a dynamic and properly funded regional policy. This will include the establishment of Regional Development Agencies (starting with the North, North-West, Yorkshire and Humberside); the promotion of local and regional enterprise boards; greater scope for local authorities to participate constructively in economic development; and creating high technology innovation centres throughout Britain.

- Create a new Ministry of Science and Technology to promote a major increase in research and development. It will co-ordinate the activities and budgets of government departments involved in these areas and will encourage, in conjunction with industry and the scientific community, the full application of science to industrial processes and products.

• Extend social ownership by a variety of means, as set out in Labour's detailed proposals. In particular, we will set up British Enterprise, to take a socially owned stake in high-tech industries and other concerns where public funds are used to strengthen investment.

Social ownership of basic utilities like gas and water is vital to ensure that every individual has access to their use and that the companies contribute to Britain's industrial recovery, for instance, by buying British. We shall start by using the existing 49 per cent holding in British Telecom to ensure proper influence in their decisions. Private shares in BT and British Gas will be converted into special new securities. These will be bought and sold in the market in the usual way and will carry either a guaranteed return, or dividends linked to the company's growth.

• Encourage the establishment and success of co-operatives of all forms.

• Strengthen the Department of Trade and Industry as the spearhead of this new national industrial strategy.

• Bring in a stronger regulatory framework to ensure honest practice in the City of London and introduce new safeguards on mergers, takeovers and monopolies to protect our national industrial, technological and research and development interests.

Plan for training

For modern, wealth-creating industry we need a well-trained workforce. British industry now carries out less than half of the training of our main competitors. Labour will therefore established a national training programme to bring about a major advance in the spread and standard of skills.

For young people we will establish an integrated, high quality Foundation Programme that will guarantee for all 16 year-olds at least two years of education, training and work experience according to their needs.

The Adult Skillplan will develop lifelong training and education for everyone needing to supplement and update skills in work, with particular emphasis given to training for women.

The Jobs, Enterprise and Training Programme will expand existing programmes for unemployed people with a guarantee of a job or new skill for the long-term unemployed.

Paying for the recovery programme

The immediate programmes will cost £6 billion a year net for the first two years.

We will pay for them by:

• Putting directly into generating 300,000 jobs the money that would be used up by the Thatcher government on its 2p income tax bribe.

• Adopting the same practice as most successful industrial countries and companies, by prudently borrowing £3 billion for useful wealth generating national investment.

We will reverse the extra tax cuts which the richest 5 per cent have received from the Tory government and allocate that money instead to the most needy. We will also bring forward other reforms to capital taxation – including the introduction of wealth tax, which whilst applying to only the wealthiest one per cent of the population, will, over the years, bring a significant contribution from those in our society best able to pay.

Alliance: Rebuilding British industry

Manufacturing and services go hand in hand, but only a quarter of services are tradeable and two-thirds of our exports depend on manufacturing. Britain cannot survive on a basis of low tech service jobs. Nor can business flourish without a thriving industry to buy their products. Manufacturing industry is the driving force at the core of our economy. Its decline must be reversed.

Therefore:

- We will introduce Industrial Investment Bonds to attractive investors into industry, a new industrial credit scheme to provide medium-term finance for manufacturing companies and a tax allowance for investment in new technologies.
- We will work in partnership with industry and put industry first. There will be a new Cabinet Industrial Policy Committee responsible for overseeing the development and implementation, in co-operation with industry, of a broad industrial strategy with long-term priorities.
- We will encourage employers to take on more staff by a 25% cut in their National Insurance Contribution payments targeted on assisted areas and areas of high unemployment.
- We will introduce a training incentive with rebates for companies who spend more money on training and contributions from those who do not provide it themselves; our new Department of Education and Training will monitor standards and turn youth training into a fully comprehensive, high quality vocational and educational programme for 16–19 years old.
- We will increase the lamentably low funding of civil research and development, placing emphasis both on commercial exploitation of new technology using the British Technology Group, and on boosting basic scientific research; we would give greater support to European Community joint research programmes.

Industrial Investment Bonds

- We will introduce Industrial Investment Bonds to liberate many new and small businesses from the high cost of borrowing start-up capital.

These bonds will help bridge the gap between the new businessman who needs access to low-cost funds and the investor, including individuals, who would like to back him or her provided the balance between risk and reward is reasonable. We will accordingly allow new and growing companies to raise funds through the issue of Industrial Investment Bonds which will pay interest free of tax to investors.

A similar scheme is already providing a valuable kick-start for many new companies in the United States. Together with the Business Expansion Scheme, our Industrial Investment Bonds will give the next generation of businesses the most favourable climate ever to build up employment for the community and profits for themselves and their investors.

Backing small business

- We will build a partnership between government, entrepreneurs and investors to encourage new businesses and create new jobs. We will especially encourage small businesses, which will be a major motor of growth and employment in the 1990s.
- We will reduce the tax and administrative burdens on small businesses.
- We will promote the establishment of Small Firms Investment Companies to provide equity and loan finance.
- We will introduce a Bill to enable business to charge interest on overdue payment of bills, if they so wish.

- We will ensure that there are business start-up schemes and expansion schemes specifically geared to encouraging enterprise by women.
- We will ensure small businesses get their fair share of public contracts from both central and local government.
- We will encourage local public/private initiatives, such as Enterprise Agencies, which we identified in our Worksearch Campaign.

Index